THE SACRAMENTS

Responding to God's loving invitation

An ecumenical course in five sessions

Jane Williams

CONTENTS

HOW TO GET THE MOST OUT OF THIS COURSE

SUGGESTIONS FOR GROUP LEADERS

We're deliberately not prescriptive, and different leaders prefer to work in slightly different ways, but here are a few tried and trusted ideas ...

1. THE ROOM Encourage people to sit within the main circle – so all feel equally involved.

2. HOSPITALITY Tea or coffee and biscuits on arrival and/or at the end of a meeting is always appreciated and encourages people to talk informally.

3. THE START If group members don't know one another well, some kind of 'icebreaker' might be helpful. Be careful to place a time limit on this exercise!

4. PREPARING THE GROUP Explain that there are no right or wrong answers, and that among friends it is fine to say things that you're not sure about – to express half-formed ideas. If individuals choose to say nothing, that's all right too.

5. THE MATERIAL It helps if each group member has their own personal copy of this course book. Encourage members to read each session *before* the meeting. There's no need to consider all the questions. A lively exchange of views is what matters, so be selective. The quotations in blue are there to stimulate discussion and – just like the opinions expressed by the audio participants – don't necessarily represent York Courses' views or beliefs.

6. PREPARATION It's not compulsory for group members to have a Bible, but it might be helpful for at least the leader to have one handy. Ask in advance if you want anyone to lead prayers or read aloud, so they can prepare.

7. TIMING Aim to start on time and stick fairly closely to your stated finishing time.

8. USING THE AUDIO/VIDEO For each of the sessions, we recommend reading through the session in the course booklet, before listening together to the corresponding session on the audio material/watching the video. Groups may like to choose a question to discuss straight after they have listened to/watched a relevant track on the audio/video – but there are no hard-and-fast rules. Do whatever works best for your group!

9. THE TRANSCRIPT, included at the end of the course booklet, is a written record of the audio/video material and will be invaluable as you prepare.

RUNNING A VIRTUAL HOUSE GROUP AND SHARING AUDIO/VIDEO

To run your virtual group, use software such as Zoom or Google Meet, and use the 'Share Screen' function to share the audio/video with your group.

PURCHASING THE AUDIO DOWNLOAD

If you would like to purchase the accompanying audio download, please go to https://spckpublishing.co.uk/the-sacraments

COMPLETE LIST OF THE SACRAMENTS PRODUCTS

The full list of available formats is as follows:

- Course book including transcript of video and access to video/audio downloads (paperback 978 1 915843 47 0)
- Course book including transcript of video and access to video/audio downloads (eBook 978 1 915843 50 0, both ePub and Mobi files provided)
- Participants' book including transcript of video: pack of 5 (Paperback 978 1 915843 52 4)
- Participants' book including transcript of video (eBook 978 1 915843 51 7, both ePub and Mobi files provided)
- Video of discussion to support *The Sacraments*, available via the course book with access to audio and video downloads
- Audio book of discussion to support *The Sacraments* (audio/digital download)

SESSION 1
WHAT IS A SACRAMENT?

A course about sacraments sounds like asking for trouble and, if it's not too much of a contradiction, really boring trouble. Sacraments are churchy things, and Christians disagree about them. That makes the prospect of spending several weeks on the subject rather gloomy. But don't give up just yet. The hope is that as we discuss sacraments, we will get a new insight into the world God loves – beautiful, even in its brokenness – and find ourselves not only refreshed, but re-enchanted.

'God is always coming to you in the Sacrament of the Present Moment.'[1]
EVELYN UNDERHILL

The letter to the Ephesians says that God tells us a great secret; a 'mystery' (Ephesians 1:9), which is that the world has meaning and purpose, and that meaning and purpose is Jesus-shaped, from beginning to end, like words through a stick of rock. *The sacraments help us enter into that mystery* not only by telling the story of Jesus, but by re-enacting it and drawing us into the action. We become part of the way in which God reveals to the world what it is for, and how much it matters. As people who carry the 'mystery' (of how God brings everything together in Jesus), we are invited to live as those who join things up, who weave things together. We are called to see the whole world and all we encounter with fresh eyes.

'I cannot help thinking that the best way of knowing God is to love many things. Love this friend, this person, this thing, whatever you like, and you will be on the right road to understanding . . .'[2]
VINCENT VAN GOGH

So, let us enjoy discovering again what it is to be a 'creature' – one who receives life as a gift, rather than as something of our own making; an embodied person, who interacts with a physical world – living, loving and learning through our senses. Let us thrill to the fact that we are only here at all because God wants us! We are not a mistake, and it's not a nuisance that we are bodily made rather than made like machines. We are human and proud of it. And that means, just as we can't get to know and understand anything in the world except through our bodies, growing in knowledge of God is a bodily thing too. God comes to meet us in our historical, physical and daily reality. The sacraments are a concentrated celebration of that.

'I would rather be what God chose to make me than the most glorious creature that I could think of; for to have been thought about, born in God's thought, and then made by God, is the dearest, grandest and most precious thing in all thinking.'[3]

GEORGE MacDONALD

---

* * *

Almost every Christian denomination recognises baptism as the means of entering into the Christian life, even if we disagree about when and to whom baptism should be offered. Nearly all Christians share bread and wine in remembrance of, and in gratitude for, God's saving work in Jesus Christ, even though we may call this rite by different names, celebrate it at varying intervals, and restrict participation in it for different reasons. And while most Christians agree that baptism and Eucharist – or Holy Communion – are sacraments, others would also include confirmation, marriage, confession, and anointing of the sick and ordination. All involve taking our lives into the story God is telling the world about its purpose.

'To be baptized is a sign that everything we are – work and play, personality and character, commitments and passions, family and ethnicity – is gathered up and given shape and definition by our identity as one of God's own children.'[4]

THOMAS G. LONG

Christianity has been called the most materialistic of all faiths,[5] not as an insult, but as a description of how God comes to find us in our actual, worldly, historical existence. Jesus teaches us to pray for our daily bread and to learn how to treat one another as sisters and brothers in the here and now. Participation is the goal rather than enlightenment. Sacraments are ordinary, daily things – water, bread, wine – enabled, through the agency of God the Holy Spirit (as we shall explore further in Session 5), to be what they are, and yet also full of the life of God.

Psalm 34:8 says

**'O taste and see that the Lord is good;
happy are those who take refuge in him.'**

However, the psalm goes on to make it clear that this is not to be a passive snuggling down into the goodness of God; rather, it's an active call to 'depart from evil, and do good' (Psalm 34:14).

'I'd rather be unhappy and know that God is with me, than be happy, comfortable and unsure of God's presence.'[6]
PETE GREIG

Sacraments are *converting encounters* – they turn us around to face God and to see one another. They are of a piece with God's character and action towards us in all that God is and does.

* * *

Let's focus more closely now on what we might understand by a 'sacrament'. There are several widely used definitions of the word, but all of them require, with differing emphases, the combination of material things and the power of God the Holy Spirit.

Augustine of Hippo, the great North African church leader and theologian, is credited with the usual definition of a sacrament, which is

---

'an outward and visible sign of an inward and invisible grace'.

Then we have Thomas Aquinas:

'the sign of a holy thing so far as it makes people holy'.[7]

The catechism of the Catholic Church:

'the actions of the Holy Spirit at work in his Body, the Church'.[8]

John Calvin:

'a kind of visible Word'.[9]

The 39 Articles of the Church of England:

'certain and sure witnesses and effectual signs of grace'.[10]

And the Westminster Confession:

'There is in every sacrament a spiritual relation, or sacramental union, between the sign and the thing signified.'[11]

What all these definitions have in common is the combination of inward and outward, visible and invisible. If you try to take them apart, you end up with nothing. Together, the outward and the inward become *active,* not just ritual but 'effective', that is, *they have an effect on us,* as all God's actions do. The visibility of the sacraments is necessary because we are seeing, embodied people. They assure us of the presence and action of God in a way that words alone could not. When we immerse ourselves in a sacrament like the Eucharist, eating the bread and drinking the wine, then it becomes part of who we are. It transforms us.

* * *

It would be anachronistic to say that in its original usage the word sacrament was 'secular', because at the time of Jesus' earthly life, the world was not seen as having religious and non-religious spheres. However, a 'sacramentum' was, among other things, an oath that a Roman soldier would take. The Roman author, Vegetius, describes it like this:

'But the soldiers swear that they shall faithfully execute all that the Emperor commands, that they shall never desert the service, and that they shall not seek to avoid death for the Roman republic.'[12]

This was a sacred oath, taken in the presence of the gods, who ensured that it was honoured; it was a binding oath, lasting a lifetime; it was an incorporative oath, making the one who swore it part of something bigger than family or race or particular nation; and it was an oath that demanded everything of the swearer, including their life.

When the Christian Church adopted the word, it saw the strength of this set of meanings. It was aware that the word was made up of the Latin word for 'sacred', *sacer*, and the Greek word *mysterion*, meaning something powerful, holy and more than earthly. In 1 Corinthians 2:1, Paul writes,

'I did not come proclaiming the mystery of God to you in lofty words'

and he continues that this 'mystery' is best exemplified in the crucified Christ, God's mysteriously wise 'foolishness', or mysteriously foolish wisdom.

Already, some of the governing principles of a 'sacrament' are coming through. Sacraments are the work of the holy God, whose holiness and power are mysteriously active in Jesus Christ, crucified and risen. As with the Roman soldiers' 'sacramentum', the Christian sacrament binds partakers into something bigger than themselves: a way of life that is communal and that cannot make sense or function if each of us individually serves only ourselves and our own needs. This bigger thing is the Church; the body of Christ. The Roman army was a ruthless killing machine that subdued peoples and used them and their resources only for the good of the Roman Empire. The sacraments of the Christian Church incorporate us into a very different empire, whose ruler lays down his life for his people. As the hymn says

**Conquering kings their titles take,
From the lands they captive make;
Jesus, Thine was given Thee
For a world Thou madest free.**[13]
CONQUERING KINGS THEIR TITLES TAKE

The two central sacraments of baptism and Eucharist invite us into this narrative. They tell us that the story of Jesus Christ is the story of God's presence and action, working for our good in a world of human violence, hatred, rejection, selfishness and stupidity. Human beings are not destroyed by the action of God; they are not forced into submission. Yet neither is the meaning of the world left in our hands, or the hope of the world shattered due to human sin, because in this real world, as we know, God acts. Sacraments are a part of that ongoing action and a demonstration of the way in which God works. Our story and God's story are really one, not two, as Tom Wright explains:

'in the Bible *heaven and earth are not far apart.* They were designed in the beginning to work together, to overlap and interlock; and they are designed in the end to come together in a rich and glorious fusion in which, as in the best marriages, each is more truly itself while being more fully united with the other.'[14]
TOM WRIGHT

We would often prefer to keep God safely in a 'religious' space, but that is not where sacraments would have us be. Instead, they call us into this world that God has made and loves, and where God is fully present.

FOR DISCUSSION

1. What problems and opportunities do you anticipate might arise from a course on sacraments?

2. Does the analogy of the Roman soldiers' oath illuminate the idea of a sacrament? If so, how? If not, why not?

3. Which sacraments does your own church regularly celebrate? Does your church talk about 'sacraments'?

4. Think about the idea that as embodied people, all our learning involves our bodies. Does that change the way we think about knowledge?

5. Is Tom Wright's description of heaven and earth as 'not far apart' familiar or new to you?

SESSION 2
GOD LOVES CREATION

The account in Genesis 1 of how God made the world is a love story. As the complex, beautiful, multi-layered world is built up, God looks at it and sees that it is good (Genesis 1:10–25). There is something of the satisfaction of any great artist here but, as we shall explore in this session, God goes further: God creates beings who *can appreciate* what has been created, who can share in it, add to it or even alter it. 'Be fruitful and multiply', God says to the human creatures who are made in his own image, 'I have given all of this to you' (Genesis 1:28–29).

Genesis 2 shows in close-up the generous intimacy that God offers the human creature:

> **'Then the Lord God formed man from the dust of the ground, and breathed into his nostrils the breath of life; and the man became a living being.'**
> GENESIS 2:7

To backtrack a little, it is notable that God has brought all the other living beings – the animals, birds, fish, plants – to life simply by speaking them into existence (e.g. Genesis 1.20 'And God said, "Let the waters bring forth swarms of living creatures . . ."'). Also, that God has not needed materials to create them – all have been made out of nothing. But now, God self-givingly breathes divine life into a creature made from the earth. Not only that, God chooses to give his human creation a relationship of interdependence, both with creation and with God.

The opening of the Gospel of John deliberately echoes the Genesis creation story with the words: 'In the beginning'. But the Gospel then refocuses the creative action of God on the re-creating action that takes place in Jesus Christ. It daringly draws us into the very being of God to help us understand why God should do such a strange thing as to bring us, and the whole of creation, into existence. Within God, John tells us, there is already self-giving creativity. God 'in the beginning', before anything else is made, is also the Word – God communicates with God and creates the world through this dynamic, loving, speaking relationship of God with God. William Barclay offers this glorious insight:

'If the word was with God before time began, if God's word is part of the eternal scheme of things, it means that God was always like Jesus . . . What Jesus did was to open a window in time that we might see the eternal and unchanging love of God.'[1]

WILLIAM BARCLAY

Genesis shows us the self-giving act of God, breathing into the human creature; John's Gospel shows us how seriously God takes that generous act, how deeply and willingly God binds divine and human life together. In Jesus, God does not just set creation going, but comes to live in creation. In other words, giving divine breath to human creatures is not enough: God goes further and invites human beings into the very relationship that God has with God.

'But to all who received him, who believed in his name, he gave power to become children of God, who were born, not of blood or the will of the flesh or the will of man, but of God.'

JOHN 1:12–13

Julian of Norwich, writing in the fourteenth century, describes creation like this:

'And in this [sight], he showed a little thing the quantity of a hazelnut, lying in the palm of my hand as it seemed to me, and it was as round as any ball. I looked therein with the eye of my understanding, and thought: "What may this be?" And it was answered generally thus: "It is all that is made." I marvelled how it might last, for it seemed to me it might suddenly have fallen into nought for its littleness. And I was answered in my understanding: "It lasteth and ever shall, because God loveth it. And so hath all things being by the love of God."'

JULIAN OF NORWICH[2]

Now, you may already be familiar with the notion of 'creation from nothing', but just to clarify, nothing forces God to create; there are no pre-existing materials that God must use to shape creation, and there is nothing lacking in God that creation supplies. Out of God's loving, creative will, God makes something that is genuinely different – not part of God, not made with divine 'matter' – but completely separate, with its own character and possibilities (like the hazelnut described by Julian), all freely given by God.

Notwithstanding the familiar challenges of everyday experience we all know so well, marvelling at the love and faithfulness of God and trusting in the fundamental goodness of creation is a wonderful starting point for a journey into the life of the sacraments. Creation is good because God says so, and God continues to enable created things to bear witness to their goodness and to speak of the God who made them. For though it may be grimy and weary, the world, as described by Gerard Manley Hopkins, remains stubbornly full of hope and potential:

The world is charged with the grandeur of God.
It will flame out, like shining from shook foil;
It gathers to a greatness, like the ooze of oil
Crushed. Why do men then now not reck his rod?
Generations have trod, have trod, have trod;
And all is seared with trade; bleared, smeared with toil;
And wears man's smudge and shares man's smell: the soil
Is bare now, nor can foot feel, being shod.

And for all this, nature is never spent;
There lives the dearest freshness deep down things;
And though the last lights off the black West went
Oh, morning, at the brown brink eastward, springs —
Because the Holy Ghost over the bent
World broods with warm breast and with ah! Bright wings.
GERARD MANLEY HOPKINS[3]

Hopkins picks up the Genesis image of the Spirit of God, the wind of God, sweeping over the nothingness of creation. Just as 'in the beginning', so now the inexhaustible life of God is at work in the world. We may only see it when it 'flashes out', but, like Julian, we know these flashes indicate the continuing, faithful, creative action of God, constantly at work, even when we are unaware of it.

The two great themes then that emerge from an exploration of the theology of creation – and that shape all sacramental life – are first, that creation is 'from nothing'; it exists only because God loves it, and says it is good. And second, in making the world and human beings in particular, God opens up a relationship of mutual love and self-giving as he comes to live a fully human life. In telling us about the character of God, the sacraments invite us to participate in that character for our own sake, but also for the sake of the world.

'Even the weakest and most vulnerable, the sick, the old, the unborn and the poor, are masterpieces of God's creation, made in his own image, destined to live for ever, and deserving of the utmost reverence and respect.'
POPE FRANCIS[4]

The sacraments joyfully acknowledge the reality that we are embodied, material, creaturely beings, and our only way to knowledge, understanding and participation is through our physicality. There is no way we can get to the spiritual without the outward and visible, and truly no reason we should want to.

Unfortunately, many religious ideas and philosophies seem to suggest that our reality is inward, or spiritual, or heavenly or intellectual. The 'real me' is not the person I am day to day, in my everyday encounters with the world, but is somehow still to be discovered. The 'real me' is not the life I am living, in which I constantly make mistakes and mess up relationships and fail to improve myself, but is somehow being held back by all the messy reality around me, and needs liberating.

'Your True Self is who you objectively are from the beginning, in the mind and heart of God, "the face you had before you were born," as the Zen masters say . . . The surrendering of our false self, which we have usually taken for our absolute identity, yet is merely a relative identity, is the necessary

suffering needed to find "the pearl of great price" that is always hidden inside this lovely but passing shell.'
RICHARD ROHR[5]

Christian sacramental theology would agree that we all need liberation and transformation, though not *out of* this world, but properly *into* it. We are called to live in loving commitment to the reality all around us. And we do this together, not as personal self-improvement, but as the people God calls to 'image' God in the world, by 'imaging' God's Son, Jesus Christ. We become part of something bigger, committed to a different way of life and a different group of people, 'because we all share in the one bread'. We find our attitude to the whole world changes.

'Do you know, I don't know how one can walk by a tree and not be happy at the sight of it? How can one talk to a man and not be happy in loving him! Oh, it's only that I'm not able to express it . . . And what beautiful things there are at every step, that even the most hopeless man must feel to be beautiful! Look at a child! Look at God's sunrise! Look at the grass, how it grows! Look at the eyes that gaze at you and love you!'
FYODOR DOSTOYEVSKY[6]

FOR DISCUSSION

1. Think through what it means for us that we are 'from nothing'. In particular, do you find it liberating or challenging – or both – to know that God does not create us because God needs anything from us?

2. Explore the Genesis picture of God breathing the divine life into the human creature, in a method that differs from the creation of all other creatures. What do you think are the implications of this, for good and ill?

3. What do you think the Gospel of John is wanting to add to the Genesis story of creation by saying that all things come into being through the Word who 'was with God' and who 'was God'?

4. Why do you think a course on the sacraments needs a theology of creation?

5. Do you think your understanding of faith has been as salvation out of this world, or salvation for the world?

SESSION 3
JESUS-SHAPED SACRAMENTS

In our last session, we explored the relationship between God and creation; in particular, we focused on the idea of 'creation from nothing'. Creation exists because God wants it, and God declares that it is 'very good'.

But the creation story leads into the sad, strange account of the break between God and human creatures, so that the natural communication between God and God's creation becomes blurred and uncertain. Genesis does not 'explain' how it is possible for human beings to disobey God and tear apart the lovely, interwoven fabric of creation; instead, Genesis simply describes the results, painting a picture of the world as we recognise it – full of violence, division and misunderstanding.

'When I was in love there was somebody in the world who was more important than me, and that, given all that happened at the fall of man, is a miracle . . .'
DONALD MILLER[1]

Although the theology of creation suggests that material things are capable of 'telling the glory of God' because God made them and keeps them in being, the theology of the 'fall' says otherwise. We no longer instinctively perceive the action of God in the world. It is true that many people find the beauty of creation to be 'numinous' – speaking of something beyond itself, though the character of this 'beyond' is not clear, and others do not see it at all.

'Ordinary things have always seemed numinous to me.'
MARILYNNE ROBINSON[2]

Some of the early Christian church leaders would likely have been in agreement with Marilynne Robinson in thinking that 'outward and visible signs' of the activity of God can be found in all sorts of places. Nonetheless, for a sign to be at all useful, it has to exist within a frame of reference that will enable us to interpret it. When you're taking your driving test, you need to study the Highway Code so that you can identify and obey the roadside signs, which would otherwise simply be distracting symbols along the way – some guessable, others not.

For Christians, the life of Jesus is the key to the sacraments. It is the life, death, resurrection and ascension of Jesus that show us how to 'read' the signs of what God is doing.

At the simplest surface level, baptism and Eucharist echo events that Jesus himself participates in and that he asks his followers to continue. Jesus is baptised in the River Jordan and, on the night before his death, he shares a meal with his closest friends and asks them to 'do this in remembrance' of him. As we participate in these actions, we are simply being obedient – for once.

'We're called to be a people known by our remembering – a remembering people. Forget to give thanks – and you forget who God is. Forget to break and give – and it's your soul that gets broken. Forget to live into . . . communion – and you end up living into a union of emptiness.'
ANN VOSKAMP[3]

At the next level of what is pointed to by these 'signs', baptism and Eucharist both draw us into telling the whole story of Jesus. We recount, not only the occasion on which he was baptised or the supper he shared with his friends, *but so much more*! Baptism and Eucharist anchor us into *a real history, in which a real person called Jesus lived and died.* After his death, his disciples kept on repeating what had happened; they went on baptising and sharing bread and wine. They did so, not out of pious nostalgia (recalling a good man, sadly deceased), but as a living and ongoing story.

In the sacraments of baptism and Eucharist, death and life confront each other and life wins!

John Betjeman's much-loved poem 'Christmas' captures perfectly both the historical reality and the continuing presence of Jesus:

No love that in a family dwells,
No carolling in frosty air,
Nor all the steeple-shaking bells
Can with this single Truth compare –
That God was man in Palestine
And lives today in Bread and Wine.
JOHN BETJEMAN[4]

And that leads us to the third level of meaning in these 'signs'. They speak about a real person, living in the history of our world, but that person is also, as Betjeman says, God. The man who was baptised by John the Baptist in the river and who broke bread and shared wine with his friends was also the one through whom creation comes into being. Reading of Jesus, the Word, being made flesh, as we did in John 1, never stops being stunning! It can wreak havoc with our notion of God, but then, as we attend, we realise that it is not so strange, after all. God loves creation. The physical world is not a mistake but beloved and chosen.

'We should be astonished at the goodness of God, stunned that He should bother to call us by name, our mouths wide open at His love, bewildered that at this very moment we are standing on holy ground.'
BRENNAN MANNING[5]

Sacraments tell us again what the world is, and who it belongs to. Sacraments reunite us with our own reality as 'creatures' – beings made out of love and for love. They do this because of who Jesus is. The great fourth-century theologian and Church leader, Athanasius, explains that the incarnation, when God the Son becomes a human being, is to do with the faithfulness of God.

'For as, when the likeness painted on a panel has been effaced by stains from without, he whose likeness it is must needs come once more to enable the portrait to be renewed on the same wood, for the sake of his picture, even the mere wood on which it is painted is not thrown away, but the outline is renewed upon it; in the same way also the most Holy Son of the Father, being the Image of

the Father, came to our region to renew man once made in His likeness, and find him, as one lost, by the remission of sins; as He says Himself in the Gospels: I came to find and to save the lost.'
ATHANASIUS[6]

We sometimes think that the Son of God becomes a human being like us, but Athanasius is suggesting something more complex and beautiful: *we human beings are a deliberate echo of the Son of God*. The Son of God brought us into being in his own image – we are his physical 'portrait' in Athanasius' metaphor. However, we have completely forgotten who and what we are, so the original of the portrait comes to 'sit' again. The whole earthly life of Jesus is the renewing of God's assurance that creation is very good, and still beloved, however much it has been 'stained'. As we share in the sacraments which draw us into the life, death and resurrection of Jesus, we might think of ourselves as a canvas, or a painting on wood, coming to be restored. And when the painting shines fresh again, we can look at one another and once more see the family likeness.

'The main theme of the Bible is the restoration of humanity and, through humanity, of the whole of creation to its original harmony.'
BEDE GRIFFITHS[7]

Only Jesus makes sense of the particular character of sacraments, because Jesus is the one who brings creation into being and then comes to live in it for its restoration. In the light of Jesus, the world might well become 'sacramental' – all kinds of things can tell the story of how beautiful, beloved and significant it is. But Jesus is the interpretation – the 'highway code' – the means by which we understand what the signs are pointing to.

Colossians 1:15–16 says Jesus

'is the image of the invisible God, the firstborn of all creation; for in him all things in heaven and on earth were created . . . through him and for him'.

All God's interactions with what God has made are 'Jesus-shaped'. God is always visible as the Jesus-shaped human response of creation to its maker.

FOR DISCUSSION

1. Do you find creation 'sacramental'?

2. Is it a new idea to you that Jesus isn't in our image but we are in his? What difference does that make?

3. This session has focused on Jesus as both really human and really God. Do you think you tend to focus more on one aspect or the other of Jesus' character? What impact do you think that has on how you see the sacraments?

4. Is it helpful to think of God as always being 'Jesus-shaped' for us? What do you think that means in practice?

5. Is Athanasius' metaphor of us as portraits of the Son a good one or not? Why do you think this?

SESSION 4
SACRAMENTS OF PRESENCE IN A BROKEN WORLD

We have seen that God made the material world out of nothing and for nothing, except to love it and share the divine life with it. We have learned from John's Gospel that everything comes into being through the Son, which reveals something fundamental about the character of creation – that it is 'filial', 'son- or daughter-shaped'. The Son becomes incarnate in the world so that this 'filial' love is fully lived out in creation. We are invited to participate, to become 'daughters and sons' of God and siblings to one another. However, after John has set out this powerful assertion about God's reality, he makes a sober and sad assertion:

> **'He was in the world, and the world came into being through him; yet the world did not know him. He came to what was his own, and his own people did not accept him.'**
> JOHN 1:10–11

In Genesis, we saw the creation story moving from the beauty and tenderness of God's interaction with creation to the chaos and violence of Cain's murder of Abel. By the time the Tower of Babel is complete, communication with God, between people, and with the rest of creation has been lost, and the world no longer makes sense.

> **'The collapse of the Tower of Babel is perhaps the central urban myth. It is certainly the most disquieting. In Babylon, the great city that fascinated and horrified the Biblical writers, people of different races and languages, drawn together in pursuit of wealth, tried for the first time to live together – and failed.'**
> NEIL MacGREGOR[1]

It is into this reality, John's Gospel says, that Jesus steps.

In the sacraments, God's active presence confronts the world's reactive resistance and rejection. Baptism and Eucharist are about death and life; in particular about Jesus' sacrificial death through which the eternal life of God pours into creation again. As we know, sacraments take ordinary earthly elements that sustain daily life – water, bread, wine – and re-enchant them. These things are gifts of God in creation, and in God's hands they are able to fill us with the life-giving presence of the God who is the world's beginning and its end. Every human story, full of brokenness and misunderstanding, joy and sorrow, is taken into the story that God tells the world of why it exists and what its purpose is. And that makes every human story still exactly what it is always was – and yet utterly different.

'May you realize that the shape of your soul is unique, that you have a special destiny here, that behind the facade of your life there is something beautiful, good, and eternal happening. May you learn to see yourself with the same delight, pride, and expectation with which God sees you in every moment.'
JOHN O'DONOHUE[2]

All the Gospels describe Jesus' baptism (Matthew 3:13–17; Mark 1:9–11; Luke 3:21–22; John 1:32–34). John's description is distinctive, with no clear mention of Jesus actually being baptised, but as with the other Gospels, Jesus' encounter with John the Baptist is a key moment of clarity, a declaration of who Jesus is and why he has come. All the Gospels recount the presence of the Holy Spirit as a dove hovering over Jesus. Matthew, Mark and Luke describe the voice of God the Father, declaring trust and love over God the Son, Jesus, as he comes up out of the waters of baptism; in John's Gospel, this is the moment at which John the Baptist knows for certain that Jesus is indeed the Messiah, the Son of God. The baptism of Jesus is a window into the eternal loving relationship of God; Father, Son and Holy Spirit – a window opened into our world, where the love of God is often so invisible to us.

Yet baptism is not a triumphal moment. At its simplest, water washes away dirt, which is what makes it such a good symbol of a deeper washing and cleansing too, the washing away of sin and shame. John the Baptist demanded that people should be baptised as a mark of repentance.

'John (the Baptist) stands as prophets do to this very day, as an unyielding presence unsettling us and leaving us not quite sure of how we feel about him.'
EUGENE KENNEDY[3]

Although ritual washing for purification was a well-known practice, John seems to have been asking something extra and unusual of the Jewish people who came to him. Normally, baptism was required for new converts to Judaism, those who had not been born into the people of God. That might explain why Matthew reports John as saying,

---

'Do not presume to say to yourselves, "We have Abraham as our ancestor", for I tell you, God is able from these stones to raise up children to Abraham.'
MATTHEW 3:9

Purifying repentance was necessary, John the Baptist says, for all, not just for those outside Judaism. John's baptism offered a re-entry into and a re-identification with, the saving work of God.

In Matthew's Gospel, John the Baptist is embarrassed when Jesus comes to him for baptism because Jesus does not need to repent or to rededicate himself to God. In Galatians 3:26–28, Paul unpacks this conundrum.

'In Christ Jesus you are all children of God through faith. As many of you as were baptized into Christ have clothed yourself with Christ. There is no longer Jew or Greek, there is no longer slave or free, there is no longer male and female; for all of you are one in Christ.'

What Jesus did in being baptised was to enter into a broken world that needs to repent and be cleansed, and confront it with the world of God's making, where all are welcomed. No one in the 'old' world can claim to have set themselves straight with God, because none of us is capable of it. But in the 'new' world, we belong to Jesus who offers us his place with God; his relationship with the Father. The natural divisions between people that keep us apart and mistrustful of one another and make us feel somewhere deep down that we are more important than others are all abolished.

'The man who is not afraid to admit everything that he sees to be wrong with himself, and yet recognizes that he may be the object of God's love precisely because of his shortcomings, can begin to be sincere. His sincerity is based on confidence, not in his own illusions about himself, but in the endless, unfailing mercy of God.'
THOMAS MERTON[4]

In baptism then, Jesus enters into the reality that John the Baptist is naming, that of alienation and distance and fills it instead with his reality of God's presence and invitation.

The same kind of dynamic is at work in the Eucharist. Its setting, of course, is the Last Supper. Jesus knows he is going to be betrayed by his friends, by his people (who will shout 'Crucify him'), by the religious leaders and by the political rulers. All those around Jesus collude in one way or another in his death. And so, too, at every Eucharist, we are the people who betray Jesus. The ritual meal that Jesus shares with his friends harks back to the story of God's action to free the enslaved people of Israel from Egypt (Exodus 12), celebrated gratefully as the Passover – when God 'passed over' the houses marked with the blood of a lamb, and death descended only on the houses of the Egyptians.

Jesus puts himself in the place of that slaughtered lamb: it is his blood that marks us as people taken out of slavery into freedom, out of death into life. As with baptism, so here Jesus enters into and accepts the world as it is, full of betrayals, enslavement and death. But he does not leave it where he found it, *he turns it round to face God.*

'I love Passover because for me it is a cry against indifference, a cry for compassion.'
ELIE WIESEL[5]

In *The Lion, the Witch and the Wardrobe*, the great lion Aslan, who is a fictional likeness of Christ, offers to die in place of Edmund, one of the human children who has come into Narnia and, through his own fault, become a prisoner and slave of the White Witch. The Witch thinks that when she has killed Aslan she has won, but Aslan rises from the dead. He tells Susan and Lucy how this is possible.

'When a willing victim who had committed no treachery was killed in a traitor's stead, the Table would crack, and Death itself would start working backwards.'
C. S. LEWIS[6]

At every Holy Communion that is what is happening: death itself is working backwards because Jesus has brought the life of God into the place of death and made it tell a different story.

In some medieval paintings of the 'Harrowing of Hell' (which is the idea that between crucifixion and resurrection Jesus visited the place of the dead), Jesus is shown, stepping lightly towards the monstrous mouth of hell, which has been forced open by his presence. The great crowds of human beings, held in captivity for centuries, begin to spill out into the light. Adam and Eve come out first, shy, still ashamed and hardly able to believe that they and all their children can be free. Eve is often shown still holding her apple; a symbol of pain and separation. But in Jesus, death is working backwards, finding itself running into the life that made the whole world and that cannot die.

In baptism and the Eucharist, we see all too clearly the reality of our broken world. But its meaning has changed, because it is now a world in which Jesus has lived, died and risen again. Everything that came into being through the Word at the beginning is coming into new being through the Word made flesh.

FOR DISCUSSION

1. If your church uses them, look at the service books it has for baptism and Holy Communion and see what they say is going on. Does it seem to match what is said in this session?

2. If you are baptised, describe when and how that happened, and what it means to you.

3. Do you find it a helpful or unhelpful idea to think of all of us gathered at the Lord's Table as the ones who have betrayed Jesus?

4. As appropriate, discuss your experience of the 'brokenness' of the world and how God seems to interact with that experience.

5. You may not be able to share Communion together, but perhaps you can promise to pray for the other members of the group next time you go to Communion.

SESSION 5
SACRAMENTS AS A PLEDGE OF THE HOLY SPIRIT

Sacraments are body-builders, in a strictly religious sense, of course. That is, they build up the body of Christ, the people of God. The two main sacraments take us very directly into the life of Jesus and the community of people that Jesus calls to be friends and witnesses. In baptism, Paul tells us, we share in Christ's death so we can share in his new life. In the Eucharist, we eat and drink Jesus' body and blood, his sacrifice made once for all on the cross, so that we who eat become 'one body'.

'We live and die; Christ died and lived!'
JOHN STOTT[1]

As I mentioned in Session 1, some traditions recognise other sacraments too, which are practised by most Christians, whether or not they are called 'sacraments'.

- Confirmation celebrates someone's decision to commit themselves to the Christian community for life.
- Confession, whether communal in a service or personal confession to a priest, welcomes back into the fellowship of the body of Christ someone whose behaviour has somehow put them on the edges or outside that community. Confession reminds us that we are still damaged and damaging people, dependent on the grace of God.
- Marriage builds a new unit within the body of Christ, with the couple both demonstrating to the gathered community something about God's faithfulness and creativity, and asking it for help in holding on to that vision.

'What marriage is for: It is a way for two spiritual friends to help each other on their journey to become the persons God designed them to be.'
TIMOTHY KELLER[2]

- **Anointing (unction) at the time of sickness or approaching death is God's gift of faithful love to our ailing bodies. Even when we are ill, our bodies are beloved by God and are capable of receiving and sharing God's grace. And when the time of death comes, we do not leave the body of Christ, but simply join it in another form.**
- **Ordination identifies a person who is called to serve the community in a particular way, and helps them to see and understand their own calling.**

These then are the seven 'body-building' gifts – baptism, Eucharist, confirmation, confession, marriage, unction and ordination. Whether named as sacraments or not, they serve the union of the body of Christ. They are not done by one person on their own. They are not only about an individual's personal faith, but also about each person's commitment to something bigger than themselves, to a relationship, or a set of relationships that exists only within the Church, the body of Christ. They are gifts for the journey, and none of them have any meaning outside the life, death, resurrection and ascension of Jesus.

But the very fact that we as Christians (1) disagree about which rites are 'sacraments' and which ones aren't, (2) disagree about what, if anything, is happening when we eat bread and drink wine during the Eucharist, and (3) are not able to share in these sacraments together across all Christian denominations tells us something sombre about ourselves as the Church. It is not only the world that is fallen and broken, damaged and damaging, Christians are too.

'To all my nonbelieving, sort-of-believing, and used-to-be-believing friends: I feel like I should begin with a confession. I am sorry that so often the biggest obstacle to God has been Christians.'
SHANE CLAIBORNE[3]

'The Christian life is not a constant high. I have my moments of deep discouragement. I have to go to God in prayer with

tears in my eyes, and say, "O God, forgive me," or "Help me."'
BILLY GRAHAM[4]

However, what really matters is this: because Jesus Christ is both fully human and fully God, God can be wholly present in everyday human reality, and God can take everyday things and transform them. Not all water is the water of baptism, and not all bread and wine are the body and blood of Christ, but these can become sacramental by the action of the Holy Spirit within the body of Christ.

In the New Testament and in Christian worship, we discover that the Holy Spirit enables the relationship of the Father and the Son, the filial relationship, to be real and active.

In Luke 1:35 the angel explains to Mary,

'The Holy Spirit will come upon you, and the power of the Most High will overshadow you; therefore the child to be born will be holy; he will be called Son of God.'

Matthew, Mark and Luke tell how, at the baptism of Jesus, the Holy Spirit descended like a dove, and the voice of God confirms that Jesus is the Beloved Son (Matthew 3:16–17).

Acts describes the gift of the Holy Spirit to the disciples at Pentecost: a gift that they instantly share with others, telling them about Jesus and inviting them into the new family.

'You will receive the gift of the Holy Spirit. For the promise is for you, for your children, and for all who are far away.'
ACTS 2:38–39

Romans 8:15–17 describes how the Holy Spirit teaches us to call God 'Abba', as Jesus does,

'It is that very Spirit bearing witness with our spirit that we are children of God . . . and joint heirs with Christ'.

The baptism service reminds us of the Holy Spirit's action at Jesus' baptism, so that we, too, are declared 'beloved children', like Jesus and because of Jesus. At the Eucharist, the celebrant invokes the Holy Spirit on the bread and wine and on the people gathered, that we may share in and become the body of Christ.

Ephesians 1:13–14 describes it like this:

'You ... were marked with the seal of the promised Holy Spirit; this is the pledge of our inheritance towards redemption as God's own people'.

That word 'pledge' is sometimes translated as 'downpayment': it is not just a future hope, but something that we partly hold now.

So then, in the sacraments, the living and active presence of the Holy Spirit, the Jesus-maker, flows through our mundane world. The Holy Spirit brings to life the loving relationship between Father and Son, lived out in our world in Jesus, and now through the Holy Spirit shared in by us. This is what we are invited into in every sacramental act as, together, we are formed into the body of Christ, the living, breathing reality of God's invitation to us to come home, to be family, to be sisters and brothers of the Son of God.

'The temple of God is the holy people in Jesus Christ. The Body of Christ is the living temple of God and of the new humanity.'
DIETRICH BONHOEFFER[5]

'Without God, we cannot. Without us, God will not.'
SAINT AUGUSTINE[6]

Of course, the action of the Holy Spirit is not confined to the sacraments. The Holy Spirit is, as the Nicene Creed says, 'the Lord, the giver of life', and in John's Gospel, Jesus likens the Holy Spirit to a wind that 'blows where it chooses' (John 3:8). But the sacraments anchor the work of the Holy Spirit in the life of Jesus. This is how we know what God is like and what God's action is bringing about. In the light of this interpretive clue, which we earlier called the 'highway code' of Christians, all kinds of things can become 'sacramental' – outward and visible signs of the inward and invisible grace of God.

Sacraments 'work' both with and without us. The Holy Spirit does not take us over and make us like automata as we enter the world of sacramental action. Just as in the earthly life of Jesus, the human and divine are not in competition and do not take it in turns to act or decide, but simply flow out as the actions and decisions of the one person, Jesus Christ.

O Holy Spirit, present throughout all creation,
be beside me in all that I do,
be between me and all that I fear,
be within me and all whom I love,
today and forever.
JOHN L. BELL[7]

We remain very much ourselves, but as we live in the sacramental world and as we relate more deeply to one another and to God, so we encounter the action of God more and more and can make ourselves at home in it so that it becomes ours too. It is not a matter of correct understanding. After all, Christians have such different ways of describing and understanding the sacraments. It is just a matter of living in the presence of God the Holy Spirit, the Jesus-maker, and knowing that we are God's family because of Jesus. It is a bit like exercise – we don't have to understand all the biology and physics of it for it to 'work'. But understanding exercise isn't the same as doing it regularly, and the latter is better for us.

'When we have the Holy Spirit we have all that is needed to be all that God desires us to be.'
A. W. TOZER[8]

In the sacramental action of the Holy Spirit, the beginning and the end come together around Jesus. God makes a world out of love. It is a Jesus-shaped world, made for the love that is between Father and Son, which is the Holy Spirit. The Son then comes to live in this world through the power of that same Holy Spirit which is given to us in the sacraments. The Church is sometimes described as a 'sign, instrument and foretaste' of the coming Kingdom of God. The sacramental life of the Church points to God, it is part of the way in which God continues to act, and it is the place where we actually 'taste and see how gracious the Lord is'.

FOR DISCUSSION

1. Do you have experience of being excluded from receiving the sacrament at a church of a different denomination? How did that make you feel? Can you understand why it happened?

2. Do you find it helpful to think of sacraments as 'body-builders' for the community?

3. What to you understand by the idea of the Holy Spirit as the 'Jesus-maker'?

4. Think about some of the ways in which you feel you encounter God outside the life of the Church. Does it help to bring these encounters into the frame of reference provided by Jesus?

5. Summarise some of the things this course has made you think about. Take time to pray for each other.

TRANSCRIPT **INTRODUCTION**

JANE Hello, and welcome to our Lent course on the sacraments. My name is Jane Williams. I'm the McDonald Professor of Theology at St Mellitus College, and I'm hoping in this Lent course to draw you into my passion for the sacraments, and what they tell us about how God reaches out to invite us into God's love and action in the world. I hope you'll feel free to disagree a bit with each other during your discussions, provided you're doing that in order to learn more and not to score points! And I'm hoping the two people who are joining me in these conversations will help to demonstrate how you can have a good conversation like this, without necessarily agreeing about everything. So, I have with me Sharon Prentis. Sharon, would you like to introduce yourself?

SHARON My name is Sharon Prentis. I'm the Deputy Director of the Racial Justice Unit at the Church of England, and our role is to support the Archbishops' Commission in implementing some of the outcomes 'From Lament to Action'. But also to support those parishes and ethno-cultural networks in order to *inhabit* our church as God fully intends! As a diverse people of God.

JANE That's wonderful, and I do hope you'll bring some of those insights into this discussion, Sharon. And we also have James Walters.

JAMES Thank you, Jane. I'm an academic and chaplain at the London School of Economics, and on Sundays I help out in a parish in north London.

JANE So, I hope this is whetting your appetite for what's to come. Thank you for joining us and we'll look forward to seeing you in the first session.

SESSION 1
WHAT IS A SACRAMENT?

JANE Hello, and welcome to the first session of our course on the sacraments. And, perhaps helpfully, we're going to start by thinking about what actually is a sacrament? But I wonder, Sharon and Jim, if you could take us back to your earliest memories of being involved in sacraments. What comes to your mind, Sharon?

SHARON I remember when I was at church, which was a majority Caribbean church, and I remember the sacraments where – we didn't have them that often actually, about once every three or four months – and it would be a very special thing, where these little communion cups would come out, and then some sliced bread. But of course, as children, we weren't allowed to partake with the adults. And it was such a sort of hushed, reverent service. And, you know, we were kind of given stares if we made any noise or anything like that.

But the adults ... often there were tears, and this kind of penitential atmosphere about taking bread and wine, taking the Eucharist, but we didn't call it Eucharist, we called it Communion. But the children were there to observe, not to participate.

JANE But you got this sense of some kind of atmosphere which was quite heavy, by the sound of it?

SHARON Yeah, it was very heavy. I think the emphasis was on how *wrong* we were as humans, as adults, and therefore adults couldn't take it without confessing. And if they took it wrongly, then there would be some repercussions. And I do remember that ... feeling quite scared about that?

JANE Yeah, let's come back to that because I think we may have lost a lot of that, for good reasons and bad. What about you, Jim, what's your earliest memory of being involved in sacraments?

JAMES Quite a contrasting experience. I grew up in a parish in the Catholic tradition in the Church of England,

and so very strong sense of the sacraments. Certainly was taught that there were seven of them in my confirmation classes, and the rhythm of the parish was what we called the Mass, the Eucharist. But I think in my childhood memories, what really sticks with me, was the sense of how this kind of worship really spoke to all the senses: the smell of the incense, the colour of the vestments, the sound of the music and everything. And so a real sense the sacred, of something, yes, mysterious, but also intelligible in the sense of kind of these are signs of God's presence here, of God's action here.

JANE What Sharon was describing, the seriousness of it, of not entering into this sacrament without repentance, did that figure at all as far as you can remember?

JAMES That was certainly a strong part of it. But I have a slightly more positive sense of a kind of delight in worship, and real celebration of the Mass and of the people of God, obeying Lord's commands.

JANE Mine are all frivolous, my earliest memories, I'm afraid. It's very shocking! I was born and baptised into the Church of South India, and my parents were ministering at the time. And my earliest memory of being involved in a sacrament – my youngest sister being baptised – I was given something to put in the collection plate. And what I was given was a twelve-sided threepenny bit, which a lot of people won't remember at all. And I swallowed it. [*Everyone laughs.*] And, obviously intending to take all the attention away from my younger sister whose moment this was and focus it on me. I won't tell you any more of that story, because it gets disgusting after that!

But that sense of being involved in celebrating something, that my little sister was being brought into a community that wasn't just our particular family, but the wider family of people, who were welcoming her and promising to help her grow up as a Christian. Which I do remember, despite swallowing the threepenny bit!

I also remember my children when they were small, exactly as you were describing, Sharon, that sense of not being able to participate in Communion. And I remember my daughter in particular, frequently holding up her hands at the Communion rail, saying, 'One for me!' And trying to explain to her why this is something you need to grow into, that particular sacrament.

I suppose we've all been talking a little bit about sacraments in our own memories, but people who are joining us on this course may be thinking, 'Well, we've always been thinking that a sacrament is a very churchy kind of thing, and not something that we really understand at all.' And these memories that we've been sharing that are about celebration but also about seriousness, how do they help people understand what a sacrament actually is, do you think? That's a tricky question, Sharon, that I'm going to pose to you! [*They laugh.*]

SHARON Well, I just had a memory of when I was about 16 and started to realise there was something profoundly serious about the sacraments. And for me at that age, the sacraments were around baptism and Communion, the Eucharist. And it was at that age when I started to seriously think about the wonder of God, and getting an understanding and a glimpse that God really loved *me* ... not just, you know, this kind of more wider notion that God loves everyone, you know. God loved me as Sharon, and with all my foibles and everything else. And this idea that I was profoundly connected to a much larger sense of God's creation as well. And that filled me with a sense of wonder. And I think there's something about talking about the wonder and the *mystery* that the sacraments allude to ... For me at 16, there was this great adventure about trying to understand what is this mysterious sacredness that God is calling me into, which is visible by these outward signs, because I was preparing for my baptism, as I came from a denomination where we had full immersion, you know. And that was like you really went under the water and came back up again! And that to me was this huge transition, this sort of rite of initiation into the church proper, even though I'd been going to the church as a child. But this was a really big thing. And the church family themselves made it a really sort of profound event as well. And I remember entering into this with my church family, thinking that this marks a transition. And so, going back to your question, Jane, I think instances where people are *invited* into this, not just those special occasions, but actually start to talk about the wonder and the mystery and the awe of God is part of that.

JANE Thank you, that's so helpful because I'm wanting to pick up quite a lot of those themes in this course, and make the sacraments feel less just churchy and something that somebody does somewhere else, and that we sort of, we as laypeople – I am a layperson myself – that we just receive and have no opinions about. And that age, 16, is a really significant age in all kinds of ways ... what's going on in the whole of your life. And to, at that point, really say, this is going to be the direction I take, these people are going to help me take it. That's a profoundly important thing to do, isn't it?

SHARON It is. It's about *identity*, isn't it? And, also knowing that you're totally accepted as you.

JANE Yeah.

SHARON You know, how do we connect people with that sense that they're loved as they are?

JANE Exactly, yes.

And what age, Jim, do you remember first taking Communion?

JAMES I was confirmed at 10. And that was still the time when you had to be confirmed in order to receive Communion. And I remember that being a very special moment. I think we had to get the bishop's permission because I ought to have been one year older or something like that. I was very keen to do it. But I did still have a sense – I grew up in a choir and singing was very much kind of the way in which I participated in worship, so there was a certainly a profound deepening of my participation in the church community after that point. But I hadn't felt excluded I don't think.

JANE No, that is very young. Did you have to sort of demonstrate that you were ready in any way at the age of 10? Did somebody ask you difficult questions?

JAMES I think I did kind of have to have a special meeting with the vicar and then certainly very rigorous confirmation preparation.

JANE I actually remember a little bit of the sermon that was preached at my admittance to Communion by a bishop whose name was Bishop, Bishop Bishop! But he was preaching on that verse from Revelation about a door opening in heaven. And I think that's always been quite key for me, that sense of giving me a vision of what I was actually participating in, where it's not just something that we as human beings do as a ritual, but it's a gift that comes from the reality of God and takes you into a different kind of world.

And as I say, as a layperson myself, and again I hope we'll go on and talk about this a bit later, I don't actually preside at Communion, I don't draw the people around the table. But I feel very strongly that those who do draw us around the table, that's what they're doing, they're drawing us, they're not doing it for us, they're drawing us around the table. So, this idea of the community that we're part of, that both of you have mentioned, has been really significant.

And I found that when I discovered that the word sacrament comes, at least in one part of its derivation, from what Roman soldiers used to take, I found that really helpful, that oath that Roman soldiers used to take that they were committing themselves to this terrible institution in the case of the Roman army, but committing themselves to it utterly, so that was going to become their life and their family, you might say. I found that actually quite helpful, helping me to realise the level of commitment that's being talked about. Which possibly brings together both what you were talking about, Sharon, the seriousness, and what you were talking about, Jim, about the joyfulness, the whole experience.

JAMES I think certainly the sense of being bound to other people is what I appreciated about learning about that definition. And the sense that sacraments are about *action*, so that the language of the tradition is one of signs, and I think we think of signs as rather sort of static things like, sort of, you know you talk about the highway code and sort of street signs. But they're signs of action, signs of what God is doing. And I think as I grew older, kind of after my confirmation, we really sort of understood more that this was a call to me to be drawn into the action of God in the world. And that was what got me excited about Christian faith, yeah again sort of later in my teens.

JANE Yeah.

SHARON It's that wonderful *public* way of being as well, and we're talking about, you know, those special services where people acknowledge this particular sign. But it's also you're not doing it as an individual, you're doing it as part of a community and that for me, that public declaration and yet also knowing that you have the support of others to journey *with* you at that key point, whether it be every week or whether it be one-off occasion, is so vital.

But I also, for me, made me realise that my understanding of sacraments was actually quite narrow as well, that there was something about the *presence* of God being with me, no matter where I was? And that there was a sacred sacramental moment as well? And it could involve reminders of when I participated in my baptism and later confirmation or I took Communion. But there was something that, almost as if there was a grace *with* me, a grace working *through* me in the activity that really resonates with me, and that's when I remember. That's when I remember because sometimes I think life crowds that memory out.

JANE But that's so helpful, that it's not just something we participate in and then leave, and leave it behind. It's something we take with us. And that again, I think it's quite countercultural, actually, this sense that this is about our personal faith, but it's also a faith that we're committed to together.

JAMES When I was growing up, people still used that phrase, 'making my Communion'. And I remember the vicar being very insistent, there is no such thing as 'my Communion', it's always 'ours', always 'us'.

SHARON I love that, I really do, because there's this idea that when we gather together it's so profound, that it isn't just an individual act, which often doesn't have any other purpose other than, sort of, I and God. But it actually is about us together.

JANE Thank you so much for joining us for this first session. We hope you will want to come back for the second one, and we'll see you there.

SESSION 2 **GOD LOVES CREATION**

JANE Welcome to our second session of our Lent course on the sacraments. This session has the title of 'God loves creation'. And it may not be obvious to everybody why that's where I wanted to really centre some of our discussion about sacraments; that they are about how God, from the very beginning, says that it's good to be a created being. And that these gifts God gives us – which I think in the Anglican liturgy, the old Anglican liturgy, I think it says at the Communion, these your *creatures* of bread and wine, your *created beings* of bread and wine – why God thinks these are good gifts for people who live in bodies and are meant to be embodied. And some people tend to think of sacraments as being *otherworldly*, taking us out of the world, whereas I'm trying to suggest they actually make us concentrate on the reality of the world.

Jim, we were just talking a little bit about why that gives us a way of honouring creation in a very particular kind of way.

JAMES Yes, and I was glad that you grounded this session in the Genesis text, because I think we're living at a moment of climate crisis, of biodiversity crisis, and as Christians, we've just simply got to go back to these fundamental questions of what are God's purposes for creation, and for all the creatures that are also non-human? And I also, I like that reference in the old Communion service that reminds us that we're not the only creatures. God has purposes for the natural world as well. And so, kind of grounding our understanding of the sacraments in what God's purposes have always been in creation, I think, is really, really important, particularly for the times in which we live.

JANE Yeah, that's helpful, and that connecting us up with the whole of the rest of creation through these very bodily signs. They're also not human creatures, they're a symbol of how we interact with the non-human, isn't it? Has this been part of your understanding of sacraments, Sharon?

SHARON I think what's really struck me is the *lavishness* and the *extravagance* of creation in general, and that, not only am I grounded in that, but it's non-hierarchical, if I can say that word, that that connection that God has facilitated gathers everything up together, in this extravagant way, and that everything is relevant. If any bit is missing, then we are all at a loss to that.

So, for me *Communion* means ostensibly an understanding, that embodiedness and that connection as well. So, it's so important to be able to appreciate and to *dwell* with that, as opposed to just entering into it and then coming away.

JANE Yeah. And I suppose people have sometimes accused the Genesis text of being a source of the way in which we exploit each other and creation. And yet there's something again about the sacraments, they're not gender-specific, they're not race-specific, they're about being created, that might enable a wider discussion there.

SHARON Absolutely. I can't enter into it, into a sort of sacrament without thinking about my siblings, human, and the wider connection to the non-human world. Because I have certain symbols and elements that remind me of that, and I do that with others as well. And so, for me that's a reminder of that.

JANE And it's a way of entering into relationship with God that very much suggests that spirituality isn't something that happens outside our bodies, from which we have to be released from being who we actually are in order to engage with God. It says something completely different, doesn't it?

JAMES I think this is a really important point that you make in the session, that one of the things that I think is very helpful about the resonances that John's Gospel has with the creation narratives, you know, throughout from, as you say, from the start with the echoes of 'In the beginning', right through to the resurrection, which takes place in a garden and the risen Lord walks in the garden just like God does in the cool of the day. And I think it's reinforcing for us a sense that the salvation that Christ brings is not just some kind of otherworldly redemption for human beings that takes us out of this world; it's happening to the *whole* of creation, it's the *renewal* of creation, it's what God has been doing from the start.

JANE And so, it's intellectual but it's also, it's whole ...

JAMES It's way beyond us as well.

JANE Whole body, isn't it? Which is why words aren't ... I love words! I'm a great one for yakking! But the sacraments remind us words don't do the whole of it.

SHARON No, I love the imagery from Psalms, which talks about not just naming specific things, but also encompasses our emotions. It encompasses so much more and points us to our saviour as well. That, you know, continue this mixture of beautiful prose and poetry, but also this earnestness of who we are in our human state keeps reminding us that we are so much more than sort of inside our own heads ... but it connects us to so much more and salvation as well! That God knows and understands the big picture. We are part of that story.

JANE We're *made* to be part of that story – that's the whole point of us really. You must often, Jim, when you're presiding at Communion and giving Communion to people, be aware that people who come and receive the bread and wine probably have totally different sets of views about what's actually going on. And you don't, I imagine, interrogate them, do you?

JAMES No, indeed, and I think it was a balance for the Church, isn't it, to work out what level of kind of understanding do we want to instil in people, so that they have a sense of reverence and seriousness that something is taking place here, while recognising that what's taking place here goes way beyond us, beyond our understanding, and beyond our immediate needs. And I think it's been interesting over the years, that the question of admitting children to Communion has really forced those questions, because people who are opposed kind of say, but children can't understand,

and then you say, well, do you understand? [*They laugh.*] So, I think it is a balance. This has meaning and again the word in John's Gospel, the Logos, is about the meaning of creation and the kind of drawing together of things into a narrative that makes sense, that we can understand, but that also transcends our understanding.

JANE I mean, I suppose the point about the meaning is partly that it is something quite serious. We are committing ourselves to a whole way of seeing the world, and shaping our characters and our decisions as a result of that.

So, in the last session, Sharon, you were talking a little bit about the seriousness and the sense of sinfulness that you remember as a child around adults taking Communion. How does that help us understand a bit more about what's going on here?

SHARON I agree with what Jim has said in terms of the service and how do you explain a mystery? And I was drawn to thinking that the liturgy draws us into that mystery, and the theology of the liturgy, what it means, the words do actually resonate with people because there are opportunities for us to be repentant, to look at ourselves and confess our sins. But to also know that we do this knowing that we are forgiven as well when that is pronounced. There is something about the rhythm that allows people to enter into that understanding. And certainly for, I think how we explain it, that how do you explain a mystery, is by being *in* that mystery, and trusting that the Holy Spirit will *unfold* it, that understanding within the community as well as the individual. So, to me that's what's so special about it.

JANE And it's an understanding that is not just what we could put on paper, that we could write an essay about, but about how we're actually then going to live. It's a lived-out understanding, isn't it? We live out together. I've got lovely memories of joining services where, in other languages – obviously I didn't understand everything that was going on but I understood the shape of this family action and was being made family as I was drawn there with others. I also have had the great privilege of participating in a signed British Sign Language Eucharist, which again was absolutely lovely because it's perfectly clear what's going on, but no words. And I don't know if you've ever experienced anything like that.

JAMES I haven't, but I agree. I think that we like a lot of words.

JANE Yes. [*They laugh.*]

JAMES In the Church of England, especially, and that just allowing our hearts and minds to kind of transcend the narrative and into a bit deeper what God is doing.

SHARON Hmm. The words are punctuated by silence as well, and the fact that we're together. There's a dynamic that goes on with that, and I too have been in services where there are diverse languages spoken. And even though you don't understand everything, you're just caught up in this kind of really dynamic way of being that can't be explained. These are almost, you know, you can't put words to it, but you understand there's something quite profound going on? And I think as a child I understood that was going on, but the emphasis slightly was on the ... the sort of contrition aspect, and the fact that we are sinful and if you took this without being properly sorry, that the repercussions would be quite profound. Now I have to say that has changed an awful lot since then. But that sense of seriousness that I've come to this, knowing that I can come as myself, come with my siblings and that God forgives and loves, it is quite profound.

JANE I suppose a lot of people feel that they don't want to bring their messiness into this sacred space. They want to almost pretend that they're different people while participating in this, and we're saying something subtly different from that, aren't we? We do bring our messiness.

JAMES Because it's about messy stuff. It's about blood and sacrifice and the pain of the cross. And so, if we're not bringing our mess, you know, how is God going to transform it in the way that has been revealed to us in Christ?

JANE And bringing our mess *together*.

SHARON Absolutely.

JANE And being willing to ... for your neighbour to know you're not perfect. Again, as part of that, you use the word siblings, which I love, Sharon ... we are made siblings in this act.

SHARON Absolutely.

You know, coming back to that point of creation, and basically how humanity has impacted hugely on our ecosystems, and the sort of adverse effects that have been wrought over the last few centuries, we start to think of not just what we've been doing to nature, but what we inevitably do to each other, because we are a global community and we see what's happening across the world. And so, it brings us back to remembrance as well, of that interconnection.

JANE I mean, that's a wonderful thing to pick up in our next session. Thank you so much for joining us for this second session and we hope that you're enjoying being a creature! See you next time.

SESSION 3
JESUS-SHAPED SACRAMENTS

Welcome to the third session of our Lent course on the sacraments. This session is called 'Jesus-shaped sacraments'. And of course, the two defining sacraments of ... that all Christians share in – baptism and Eucharist – arise directly out of the life, death and resurrection of Jesus Christ, who was a real person, who really lived and really died. And how much of that do you think comes across when we're participating in sacraments, that focus on Jesus?

JAMES I think it's easy to forget, isn't it? And actually, we're told to remember! I think as I was reading this session, Jane, it really made me think of my pilgrimages to the Holy Land, because that connects you with this person who lived and died and did all these things. And for me, the Holy Land is sacramental in the sense that I think it continues to radiate the miracles that were performed there. And of course, the ultimate miracle of the resurrection. I've taken many groups and I think it's a place where people can really have sort of transformative experience in particular of celebration of the sacraments.

JANE Mmm. That's fascinating. I know for a lot of people that sense of a place being sacramental, being a way in which we engage with God is, is profoundly important. Have you been to the Holy Land?

SHARON I have indeed.

JANE Yeah.

SHARON It's, again, had a profound sense of encountering ... this was the place where *Christ walked*!

JANE Yeah.

SHARON This was, purportedly, you know, what happened here, and the old streets of Jerusalem as well. Walking around the old streets actually resonated with me. And having this sense, a profound sense of the *reality* of Christ. And I think much more than normal in terms of my relationship *with him* as a person. But this was where he was, the people that he associated with were, and that for us, I think it brought us to this embodied experience, quite emotional, actually.

JANE There's something about looking at a piece of water, the Sea of Galilee, that you knew Jesus saw. It did bring home something of the, of the reality of this human person who lived in a particular place at a particular time, and something very moving about the place where he was probably crucified. This is a place that saw something that should have been impossible: the death of somebody who embodies God. But that's such a mind-blowing idea, isn't it?

JAMES And people don't always find that easy in the old city of Jerusalem, because it's a very different environment to our quiet little churches, uh, you know, and particularly when I've taken groups on the stations of the cross ... and normally if you do that in a parish church, it's very, very quiet. And, you know, we're just there with our prayers. You're going through the, the souk, the market, and it's very chaotic and it's very noisy and it's as it would have been just before the festival, before Jesus' death.

JANE And of course, still a place of great conflict ...

JAMES Absolutely.

JANE ... as it was at the time. So, it's not a nice cosy thing that we're entering into when we tell the story of Jesus.

JAMES Absolutely.

SHARON Sometimes we sanitise Jesus, don't we? Jesus Christ to the extent where ...

JANE Gentle Jesus, meek and mild ...

SHARON Exactly! And I can't sing that to be honest. And, you know, there are certain images that come to my mind of growing up – of Christ, which was ostensibly not the images that I was formed in, or socialised in. Jesus was either white or had blonde hair and blue eyes. And the Holman Hunt picture, Jesus ...

JANE Of *The Light of the World* ...

SHARON ... *The Light of the World* comes to mind in that respect. And I remember thinking, I could never be like that. Not just the physical appearance, but everything that it kind of portrayed, this kind of innocence and quiet gentleness and in a human way.

And that's why I really want to be careful because I've come to realise that my relationship with Christ enables me to cultivate the fruits of the spirit in ways that I can totally inhabit as me. And that Christ's presence with me is not just as someone who is loved, but someone who the very best of who I can be in Christ comes forth. And I love the way that Paul writes about, you know, Christ in me, the hope of glory to come. But also that I am in Christ as well. So, not only there's Christ in me, but I am in Christ too! And that fills me with this sense of ... actually, all those images from my past or what have been projected on me, are not the real image of Christ. When I enter into a sacramental moment, I have a sense of who I am.

JANE That's such an important point, isn't it? I mean, we keep making Jesus in particular in our own image, and because so much of the image that we've grown up with has been Western artists, it's really significantly diminishing our understanding, isn't it?

JAMES I mean, I think it's true for all of us that if we were there two thousand years ago, we would find Jesus much stranger than we think we would! It's one of the things I like about Pasolini's film, *The Gospel according to St Matthew*, where Jesus is quite a difficult figure in that, uh, and it's, the script of the film is simply the Gospel of Matthew, but Jesus' manner is quite alien, it's quite hard, and I think it's important for us to be confronted with that and challenged by it.

JANE And I think in this session I talk about the great fourth-century theologian Athanasius, who in his wonderful book about why God had to become a human, he reverses what a lot of people think. We think Jesus became human so that Jesus could find out what it's like to be us. But actually, Athanasius says it's completely the opposite. Jesus becomes human so we can find out what it's like to be a human being, one who's actually in connection with God. So, it's a discipleship pattern that's going on in these sacraments isn't it? And it's actually saying, you come as you are. But you don't leave as you are. You leave as more, or more connected, more challenged, more encouraged to grow and change. I don't know if that makes sense?

SHARON Yes. I think the wonderful thing about coming as we are is that we can be totally honest. And we can bring, um, we talked about our messiness. The world is messy. We are messy. We bring that honestly, and there's an authenticity and integrity to that that is fully accepted. But in bringing that and having that encounter – because it is about encounter – we not only see ourselves as who we are, but what we can become ... because we have the opportunity to enter into grace. And I think that's a powerful thing. It's a powerful statement that we not only own but take with us back into our lives.

JANE We often talk about inviting Jesus into our life, as though it's our life, and we kindly open that door, you know, that Jesus is standing outside knocking. This is sort of saying the opposite, isn't it? That God is kindly inviting us into God's life. That we've broken ourselves up in all kinds of ways and sort of forgotten what human beings are, because human beings are people built to be in relationship with each other. We've lost such a lot of that. And so, this idea that actually sacraments are inviting us into God's life, which doesn't make us less human, but more human, that's, I find that an obviously, a helpful idea as I've written about it.

JAMES I find it helpful to remember that Jesus calls us to remember in the Eucharist, and the opposite of remembering is dismembering, is kind of separating things, is cutting things off, cutting ourselves off from our responsibility for the poor, cutting ourselves off from creation, cutting ourselves off from one another. And what's going on in the Eucharist and in the sacraments is being made more human by being remembered by God and participating in that through our own remembering.

JANE That's really helpful, that remembering idea.

SHARON And it's about also remembering the possibilities of the kingdom, the creation of what will be. But is also *now*! I think sometimes we forget there's so much difficult, challenging news at the moment. And, you know, you can feel overwhelmed by all that and you feel that you can't do anything. But coming together, we realise that actually, the hope of Christ is evident in what we're doing together, but also, we can take that with us and speak missionally to another possibility. And that's exciting.

JAMES And that is the gospel. And to come back to the Holy Land, I had the great privilege of presiding at a Eucharist with some pilgrims in the chapel attached to an orphanage in Bethlehem. And we'd spent some time with the children before, and many had been orphaned in the conflict; many had learning disabilities, and you know, it was really quite desperate, and we were all really quite tearful.

And then, of course, you know, we were there in Bethlehem and you think, well, you know, two thousand years ago, someone looking into that stable would kind of think, you know, poor tyke, not much hope for him! But God was at work. And as we celebrated the Eucharist in that orphanage, I had a very strong sense that God was at work here among these people, among these children.

JANE And so, one of the things that really comes through in sacraments is, I mean, that extraordinary thing that we keep saying, that God becomes human. These two things that are logically separate, God is able and willing to enter into the reality that God has made in order to participate with us in that actual reality.

And for all kinds of people, that sense of the presence of God in the reality that we actually inhabit has been profoundly important, particularly perhaps at times of crisis. I don't know if you've experienced that yourself? I mean, that's where you told us from Bethlehem. That's one of those, isn't it? And God doesn't wait till we've got things right before God will come and join us.

SHARON Absolutely, absolutely. I live with chronic pain and, um, one of the things that I found is that when I am entering into this sort of sacramental way of being, not that I forget my pain, but there is something that ... It's quite profound that happens in that ... I am enabled to see a bigger picture, not to explain to people and then dismiss it, but understanding that I am not alone in this ... understanding that one day things will be transformed; understanding that I have a Saviour who died and rose again and brings me the possibility of something else. And then I have an affinity with my sisters and brothers who might be navigating all sorts of pains, but I don't purport to be able to say to them, be dismissive about it, but to walk alongside. And certainly, as an ordained priest, I think there's so many things about our human condition that, when we are aware of it, we understand actually that we are being formed as a continual sense of being formed into Christ. And that's a profound thought. And that enables us to continue, really.

So those times when we have almost glimpses of the mysterious, the heaven, that we can't articulate ... are part of that formational process, becoming more like Christ.

JANE I mean, that's really helpful because it's talking about the reality that God has taken seriously enough to enter. But anything God enters, it's not going to be left in the same ...

JAMES It doesn't stay the same.

JANE Yeah.

SHARON Yeah, absolutely.

JANE And so, that sort of transformational element that we're committing to being part of, and looking forward in hope as well as looking back with gratitude.

There's a quote in the book from Ann Voskamp when she says, 'If you forget to give thanks, you forget who God is. If you forget to break and give, and it's your soul that starts to get broken.' And that sense of this gratitude at the heart of the sacrament, again, that we're being given something that is not just what we could do for ourselves.

JAMES You spoke at the beginning of the course about the sacrament of the present moment, and I think the sacraments are forming us into this, not just these actions that we continue to carry out in our daily lives, but a disposition, a way of living. And I think it is eucharistic. It is profoundly thankful, thankful for what we have been given, but thankful for the hope of transformation.

JANE And that's a good jumping-off point for our next session. So, we'll say thank you for joining us for this one and please come back for the next one.

SESSION 4
SACRAMENTS OF PRESENCE IN A BROKEN WORLD

JANE Welcome to the fourth session of our Lent course on the sacraments. And this session is called 'Sacraments of presence in a broken world'. And I think one of the things I was trying to look at in this particular session was that obviously sacraments are a source of joy and hope, but they're only that because they're realistic about the world that we actually live in. They're profoundly realistic stories about how human beings treat the gifts of God, which in Jesus' case is, we kill him.

Sharon, you really graciously and generously at the end of our last session talked a little bit about what it's like to live in pain, and how sacraments are a way of entering into that pain truthfully and realistically, but not as though it's the end. Are you willing to talk a little bit more about that?

SHARON Yes. Um, at one point I never used to want ...

JANE I know ...

SHARON to talk about it to anybody because I felt, I felt, you know, I had to be stoic.

JANE Yes. So, are you happy to do it now?

SHARON Oh yes, I am completely, because I think that shows how my understanding has been transformed in itself. And there's something about entering into the sacramental presence, or partaking in the Eucharist, that says something about our story, as related to Jesus Christ's death and resurrection. And so, there's something very real for me. And actually, I thought, at that point when I decided I'd speak about it, that as a community of faith, there needed to be a degree of honesty and openness, because that's how we present ourselves ... to God ... in these moments.

And whatever is difficult and messy has the ability to become sacred, as we bring them. And so, for me, being honest about my journey, being honest about what is happening, and how that is changed and transformed, not just changed, but transformed – doesn't mean it goes away ...

JANE No.

SHARON That we enter back into the extraordinary circumstances of our lives, but with almost a different grace, a different way of being, a different grace, a different way of being, I think ...

JANE That's so helpful to me because they're not a magic wand. God doesn't do magic.

SHARON No, no.

JANE God works with the reality in a way that is really transformative. As a teenager, as so many teenagers do, I suffered from anorexia. And again, I found engaging in sacraments when I really didn't want to eat anything – in case it made me *massive* – profoundly important. That sense of being a beloved body, even my, even though my body was something I wasn't sure that I loved at the time, being enabled to take that embodiedness and the brokenness of it and the messiness of it into that particular sacrament was hugely significant. And I think part of the way in which I finally began to grow up – and like you, I very seldom talk about that because it feels, in retrospect, such a weird thing to have suffered from – but it is part of who I am and has shaped my attitudes in all kinds of ways.

And so that idea that God doesn't *undo* the past, but equally makes the past tell a different story. Do you find that a helpful image?

JAMES Yes. I think what we're talking about is the way in which sacraments provide us a framing for our reality, that takes it very seriously. It's brokenness and it's pain, whether that's pain in our own lives, or the pain of creation, the seriousness of the climate emergency. But not despairing. Enabling us to look at those things with seriousness and no fear, seeing the possibilities of transformation, seeing God at work within that and trying to connect with that.

JANE And I just, I think so many people would quite like,

well, we all would, wouldn't we, God to wave a magic wand and just make everything different. And this is such a different approach that you don't know the meaning of something until it's fulfilled, until it comes to the end. So that the lives that we're living are en route, they're not arrived yet. And that the final meaning of creation and our involvement in it with each other is something that is still in God's hands. God gives us the world, but not in a way that can ultimately change its purposes. And the sort of sacramental hope is a big part of that for me.

SHARON Absolutely.

JANE I mean, one of the images I use, which is an image I discovered quite by accident, is an icon of what's usually called the harrowing of hell, which is between his death and resurrection. Jesus went down to the place of the dead. And so that the life and action of God in Christ works backwards as well as forwards. So, all the people who died before the coming of Christ are also enabled to be part of ... it's actually, it's particularly that image of Eve stepping out of hell's mouth, carrying her apple ... as though, you know, all through this millennia, she hasn't been able to let go of what she did, with the consequences that came.

JAMES It's a wonderful image. And I think particularly those ones where Jesus seems to be kind of dragging them, you know, that actually we are talking about the agency of God, not our own agency. You know, this is receiving what God is doing.

JANE Yeah.

SHARON And doesn't that bring us back to this mystery, which is encapsulated by the word 'sacraments', you know, as both symbol and sign, meaning and purpose, but also essentially mystery too.

And, and so we don't have to explain, because we want to have a degree of understanding of what we're doing, but actually it's so much more than our understanding even. And, and that means we have to let go to some extent. I had, um, this beautiful image. Uh, I remember being in a church with a, a group of small children. They teach you so much, do children! [*Sharon and Jane laugh.*] And, um, there was a 2-year-old who had all her teddies and dolls placed around her, and she was giving them some biscuits, and ... I was just curious as to what she was saying, because it was the same thing. And she was saying, 'And this is for you', 'And this is for you', 'And this is for you'.

And what she was doing was actually just reflecting what she'd seen. And it really struck me that, again, the generosity of God and this child *understood* this act that had happened, that she'd seen, 'And this is for you'. And I just thought, 'Yes, and this is for me.' That God's grace is for me.

JAMES Sounds like a vocation there!

SHARON Exactly! I should go back and find out. But yes, that understanding was engendered at such a young age. And that's beautiful.

JANE Yeah. Obviously, our times when we're offering them at times of severe crisis, or indeed end of life? We're saying something about the ongoing possibilities of a life that seems to be, as far as we can see, ending. I don't know if either of you have had such a privilege of being with somebody at such a point?

JAMES Certainly. I think most clergy have the experience of administering the last rites. I also baptised a young person on his deathbed. He was a PhD student, mid-twenties, had this shattering, sudden diagnosis of stage-four cancer in three major organs, had very ... had a few months.

And we met up and talked over that time, and he shared a bit of how he was feeling, and I shared a bit of the gospel, what I thought God might be saying or doing in, in this sort of dark situation. And he went into hospital and then I got a phone call, saying that he'd like to be baptised and, and I came in.

I asked the nurse for a bowl of water, but all she ... the only thing she could find was a bedpan! [*Jane laughs.*] So, so we baptised him out of this, uh, bedpan. And the curious thing about that deeply humbling privilege was, it must have been about the middle of the afternoon, but in my mind as I look back, and at the time it felt like the dawn. It felt like a dawn was breaking, the dawn of the resurrection, and that the terror of death was receding. It was very beautiful.

JANE How profoundly moving, yeah.

SHARON I think to be with somebody at that time, you realise then when you, uh, as an ordained priest, that there is something else going on and, you know, something quite profound. It's a very special time. And I too have had that privilege. And I think what has struck me was it's not just yourself and the individual and maybe the family members, but there's a real sense of the presence of God with you all at that moment. It's an enormous privilege, isn't it?

JAMES You know, what does Jesus kind of continually say in the gospel, 'Do not be afraid', Do not be afraid.'

And at these moments where we confront really difficult things – our own mortality, untimely death – it's a great privilege to ... it's useful to have these signs to reach to that help us to navigate that, but then those signs take over and they speak to us and they say, don't be afraid.

JANE And I know too how people have found anointing when they're very ill and approaching the end profoundly important, as though you are able to say your body is still beloved. It may not be functioning as you would like it to. But it doesn't make it incapable of bearing the presence and action.

JAMES And it's a great sign of dignity. Often, death isn't easy, and hospitals aren't nice places to be a lot of the time. But this sense of being anointed with sacred oil gives an enormous sense of the dignity of the person, of the body, that this is a beloved child of God, whom God is about to receive. And that's the truth.

JANE One of the many things that's so beautiful about what you just told us, Jim, was strangely, you were given a gift of hope.

JAMES Absolutely.

JANE At that time, you were there to minister to somebody

else, but, but received yourself at that time. And again, that sense of this always being something we do together comes through very beautifully, there, doesn't it? It's not, we don't do this to other people. We do it together. That idea that I'm trying to work with in this course, that what God is always doing is inviting us into the relationship that God has with God. And that what's going on in the sacraments is a little tiny bit of a mirror of that. I don't know if you've got ways that will help people picture that when they're doing this course?

SHARON I love that wonderful image, there's that icon, isn't it? Is it Rublev's icon?

JANE Of the Trinity.

SHARON Of the Trinity. And I always imagine it as a very dynamic picture of this sort of, there's this wonderful dance. There's that funny word, perichoresis, isn't there? This, this actual dance where you're invited into that as well. And I just find that really comforting. But also, strangely inspiring and awe-making as well that we're invited into this. And the invitation that is generous and extravagant and is very much shaped from who we are as well. You're not required to be X, Y and Z, but ostensibly who *you* are. This invitation is open to you. And that, for me, is wonderful.

JANE And then that you become part of the invitation to other people. Yeah. Yeah. Wonderful. And again, you two are so brilliant at this. This is a really good place to take us into our final session. So please do join us for the next session when we are looking at what it is to be community.

SESSION 5
SACRAMENTS AS A PLEDGE OF THE HOLY SPIRIT

JANE Welcome to our fifth and final session of our Lent course on the sacraments. And this one is called 'Sacraments as a pledge of the Holy Spirit'. And in this, I particularly wanted to explore, I mean, obviously when you're doing a baptism or presiding at a Holy Communion, you invite the Holy Spirit to come and make those ordinary elements into something that carries the presence and action of God. And that can come across as a kind of magic. Whereas actually, I think I want to say what's always happening is that the Holy Spirit is trying to make us into the body of Christ, make Jesus more visible and build this body.

Now I'm a layperson, um, I participate in sacraments, but I don't invite people and draw them around the sacramental action. What's it like to draw the people into such an action? And is that what you feel you're doing when you're, say, presiding at a Holy Communion?

SHARON I think there's something about being prepared for that and the sort of awesomeness of almost enabling your siblings to be a part of this as well. And so, the preparation's important, but also the sort of profound reality that it's not about you at all! [*Laughs.*] It's about how do you enable, support, affirm the community to enter into an encounter, which is quite a profound one as well.

I remember one of the occasions where I've presided, and somebody brought in a loaf of homemade bread. And so, you know, we consecrated this. But what we did was we physically handed it around ... People broke off as not just a sign of the body of Christ, but that we were part of a body as well. And so, you know, it might be slightly different to how people normally do it. But it was seeking ways to enact and to remember that we were part of a community. And that by being together, that we were fed individually, but fed together as well.

So yes, it's, er, profoundly awesome, to be able to do that.

JANE Yeah, absolutely. We can talk about it as though it's something the priest does, can't we? Rather than something that we do together. I don't know what your experience is of how people see you when you're presiding at the Eucharist, Jim?

JAMES I like the language that you've used through this course of invitation. I think, um, I see my role as the one of invitation, the role that Jesus takes in saying, come and see. And then holding the space for people. And I think a lot of that, you know, can be quite mundane and you're kind of thinking, um, you know, where have I left my sermon text? Or why is no one giving a hymn book to that person who's just arrived? Or whatever ...

But you know, then there are moments when you look out at these people, who are gathering around this altar, often *extremely* diverse, and that's been the case sort of since the early church when slaves were receiving Communion alongside slave owners. This is a transformative, uh, this is very countercultural, and it's those moments where I kind of stand there, and I just kind of think, wow, what an enormous privilege this is to do this. And I think that is how the Holy Spirit, as well as doing something special with these elements, the Holy Spirit is coming upon the people of God and making them the Communion of Saints.

JANE Yes. That's such a lovely image, isn't it? I've found the first time I saw a woman presiding at the Holy Communion – because I'm that old that when I was growing up, women weren't allowed to do that – first time I saw a woman presiding at the Communion, it was, again, it's what you were talking about, Sharon, the images and stereotypes that we've been fed, I suddenly thought, Oh! It's a family table! You think, well, that all that imagery is there. Why have I never seen it before? Because I'm more used to seeing a mother, you know, setting out to the table. It was extraordinarily important. And I'm now able to see that whoever's doing it, it's a family table that we're invited to.

I don't know if you've got particular experiences of when you could visibly see a community being built by sacramental action in some way. We could see this body-building aspect happening?

JAMES I was part of a community about twenty years ago after I graduated, which was a similar kind of church to the one I grew up in, in terms of its rituals and its churchmanship. But it was just a central London, very, very much more diverse community. And about twenty percent of our congregation were people seeking asylum in the UK.

And it was around the period where some of the really harsh rhetoric about asylum seekers started to come in. I think it's got a lot worse now, but it was kind of creeping up then. And I just remember, as I sort of stood in the queue to go up to receive Communion next to these people, just as we said in the first session, feeling bound to them, feeling this very strong sense of identity, that maybe isn't reflected in national identity, but is present in the body of Christ. And that had a profound impact on me and the role that I think the Church plays in fostering a community that we just don't normally see.

JANE Yeah, and that's not one of just people we've chosen to be with ...

JAMES Absolutely ...

JANE ... but people God has chosen to be with us.

SHARON Absolutely. And there's also one of the things that we then become aware of ... is who's missing.

Not just who is part and parcel there, but, you know, whether it be somebody who is ill, or whether it be not reflective of the wider demographic. Or whether it's about something that we are being called to do, to be a part of, we start to see in a different way, I think. And it's not just about familiarity. It's about what is God not just doing amongst us, but what are we being led to be attentive to? I think that happens as well. And I certainly have experienced that as part of a community where we, where we've gathered around the Communion table. And then, you know, in our conversations afterwards, or certainly, you know, maybe we've been doing a Bible study and we've thought, actually, we are being called to pay attention to those on the fringes or much more ... or within our congregation, or something that we need to do to address in terms of our building up of ourselves, and our formational ways of being. 'Cause we think of formation as being individual, but it's also corporate. And that has been as a result of sharing in Communion.

JANE There's all those stories that Jesus tells about banquets, aren't there, where usually the people who think they ought to be there either can't be bothered or are told to sit somewhere lower, and people are sent out to invite people who aren't there. I mean, it is a, you really brought out the sort of missional aspect. We should be looking to see who hasn't had their invitation, who doesn't know there is an invitation. And again, that isn't always how people see it. 'Cause it can seem like a something for insiders only.

JAMES Yeah, and I think it's a balance that we talked about in earlier sessions in terms of there's some requirements for entry. This is a binding. It is the, you know, the vow that we're talking about. But God's grace is for everyone, and we have to show that. So, I think one of the ways in which Church of England does that in particular is through sacrament of marriage, you know, where if you're English and you want to get married in church, you know, we do it. And I think it's a profound experience for people.

And then thinking about those moments where a sacramental action can reach out to someone. And what comes to my mind is several years ago, we had a homeless man who hung around the church, and I got involved in his story in various ways and then lost touch with him. And several years later, he just turned up! And he was looking very much kind of smartened up. It was really encouraging. He'd obviously been able to address his addictions and, and so forth. And he handed me fifty pounds. And he said, I've come to give this back. Several years ago, the sacristy door was open. You were looking away. I stole it from the church. And I realised he was doing his twelve-step programme, and this is part of his kind of reconciliation. And so, it was very important that I did receive that money, even though part of me was kind of wanting to say, well, you need it more than we do. So, I took it back.

But I said to him, well, you've just made a confession. I'm a priest. Would you like me to give you absolution? And he said, well, what's that? And I said, well it's a sign through the Church that actually God completely forgives you for this. So, I did. And it was very, very moving. And I think it was ... lost touch with him since, but it felt like a way of drawing people in really from the margins.

SHARON That is so significant, isn't it? For people to know that they're forgiven. I think it just releases people into, you know, who they can be. Because there is, there isn't that opportunity really in our everyday lives to kind of be totally honest with somebody else and say, this is who I am. I am remorseful.

I want to make amends for it. How can I do this? And, you know, just that simple act of saying that God sees and forgives you can release people into a different way of being ... the whole sacrament of reconciliation, because that's in effect, what we're entering into is quite a profound one. And I've just finished a retreat for those being ordained deacons and priests. And this is not normally part of the majority's church tradition. But a significant number wanted to enter into that sacrament of reconciliation, because they wanted to be totally honest before God and somebody else. And what struck me was this desire to say, Lord, you know who I am. You know, the totality of what I've done, but I am stepping out into a different way of being by your grace. I just found that profoundly moving. And at the end of that particular liturgy, the priest that does that, it says, and also pray for me a sinner, which, you know, it brings it right down that we are doing this together. This is not just about me, you know, just sort of ministering to you. But I also realized that I need God's grace.

JANE And that's such a lovely story of exactly what I was hoping people might begin to look at, this idea of building a body that isn't just our best friends, but is a new way of being human together. You were reminding us, Jim, that in the early church, all kinds of people would be coming together who never would, under any other circumstance, have been in the same room with each other. Slaves and free, women and men, Jews and Gentiles, and that there ought to be something a bit subversive about the Christian community. So that's a little bit of a challenge that I'd love to leave people with in this course.

I think people entering at the beginning of this course – it's a course about sacraments – and might've been expecting us to talk a bit more about the fact that as Christians, there are many sacraments we can't share across different denominations and traditions and that we have slightly different theologies of what's going on in the sacraments and all of that.

And we've instead tried to look much more at what it tells us about God and about who we are. And obviously people sharing this course may not be able to break bread together. They may not come from the same denominations. Is this theology just sort of saying 'There, there'? Let's not worry about divisions, or is that, can it do a bit more?

JAMES I think we live in an age where we focus a lot on individual and individual faith, and it makes questions of order quite frustrating and difficult to understand. And it is very difficult when you, for me, to visit a Roman Catholic church and know that I shouldn't receive communion, and ... But, I think we can't shy away from these challenges and these conversations that need to happen. What I think, I hope we've done in this course is maybe try to sort of shift the language a little bit away from the conventional disagreements towards the shared question, to get back on my hobby horse, so pressing in the climate crisis, biodiversity crisis of, what is God doing in creation? What is God doing in the world? And how does our worship show us signs of those transformative actions that we can participate in? And my experience is you can have incredibly fruitful ecumenical conversations on those terms.

SHARON I agree with you completely, Jim. And I think there's some, something about understanding the presence of God amongst us. And though for, you know, tradition, history, reasons to do with that, there are these discussions around that ... But this sense that we are called by God and loved by God, and given a grace to be able to connect across, across boundaries and have a sense of this shared fellowship, even though we might not be able to partake in the same way. And that God is still *doing* something is so profound.

I remember going to an Orthodox church and just being, sort of really felt that keenly. But also felt the hospitality of my sisters and brothers as well afterwards. And I mean, I can't explain why there are these certain divisions, but I know that people's hearts are about how we are part of this larger family and this bigger story.

JANE Thank you, Sharon. And thanks to all of you who've joined us for this course. Our hope and prayer is that you have been extending that hospitality to each other in the ways that we're able to, and that you have found this helpful. I do want to thank Sharon and Jim for participating in these conversations and for all of you who've been part of them.

NOTES

SESSION 1 WHAT IS A SACRAMENT

1 Evelyn Underhill, *The Letters of Evelyn Underhill* (Oxford: Benediction Books, 2008).
2 Vincent van Gogh, Letter to Theo van Gogh, written July 1880 in Cuesmes. Translated by Mrs Johanna van Gogh-Bonger, edited by Robert Harrison, number 133.
3 George MacDonald, *David Elginbrod* (London: Hurst and Blackett, 1863).
4 Thomas G. Long, *Accompany Them with Singing: The Christian funeral* (Louisville KY: Westminster John Knox Press, 2013).
5 William Temple, *Readings in St John's Gospel* vol. 1 (Harrisburg PA: Morehouse Publishing Company, 1985).
6 Pete Greig and Dave Roberts, *Red Moon Rising* (Eastbourne: Kingsway, 2004).
7 Thomas Aquinas, *Summa Theologica III*, q. 60, art. 2.
8 *The Catechism of the Catholic Church*, Part Two, Section 1, Chapter 1, Article 2, I The Sacraments of Christ.
9 See https://jasongoroncy.com/2010/02/15/thinking-with-calvin-about-the-relationship-between-pulpit-font-and-table/ (accessed 1 August 2024).
10 See https://www.sevenwholedays.org/2011/04/07/article-xxv/ (accessed 1 August 2024).
11 See https://www.apuritansmind.com/westminster-standards/chapter-27/ (accessed 1 August 2024).
12 See https://en.wikipedia.org/wiki/Sacramentum_(oath) (accessed 1 August 2024).
13 Words: Unknown author, in the Paris Breviary, 1736, for the Feast of the Circumcision at Second Vespers (Victis sibi cognomina). Translated from Latin to English by John Chandler, *Hymns of the Primitive Church*, 1837.
14 See https://www.fulcrum-anglican.org.uk/articles/standing-on-the-fault-lines-the-dangerous-joy-of-sacramental-life/ (accessed 1 August 2024).

SESSION 2 GOD LOVES CREATION

1 William Barclay, *The Gospel of John: Volume 1* (Edinburgh: Saint Andrew Press, 2009).
2 Julian of Norwich, *Revelations of Divine Love* (Oxford: OUP, 2015).
3 Gerard Manley Hopkins, 'God's Grandeur' in *Poems and Prose* (London: Penguin Classics, 1985).
4 See https://www.ncronline.org/news/vatican/pope-elderly-sick-unborn-poor-are-masterpieces-gods-creation (accessed 10 September 2024).
5 Richard Rohr, *Falling Upward: A Spirituality for the Two Halves of Life* (London: SPCK, 2013).
6 Fyodor Dostoyevsky, *The Idiot* (London: Penguin Classics, 2004).

SESSION 3 JESUS-SHAPED SACRAMENTS

1 Donald Miller, *Blue Like Jazz: Nonreligious Thoughts on Christian Spirituality* (Nashville TN: Thomas Nelson Publishers, 2003).
2 See https://lareviewofbooks.org/entitled-opinions/marilynne-robinson-perception-ordinary/ (accessed 12 September 2024).
3 Ann Voskamp, *The Broken Way: A Daring Path into the Abundant Life* (Grand Rapids MI: Zondervan, 2016).
4 John Betjeman, 'Christmas' in *A Few Late Chrysanthemums* (London: John Murray, 1954).

5 Brennan Manning, *The Ragamuffin Gospel*, rev. edn (New York: Crown Publishing Group, 2005).
6 Athanasius, On the Incarnation of the Word, 14, *Church Fathers: On the Incarnation of the Word* (Athanasius) (newadvent.org) See https://www.newadvent.org/fathers/2802.htm (accessed 12 September 2024).
7 Bede Griffiths, *A New Vision of Reality: Western Science, Eastern Mysticism and Christian Faith* (London: HarperCollins, 1989).

SESSION 4 SACRAMENTS OF PRESENCE IN A BROKEN WORLD

1 See https://www.theguardian.com/artanddesign/2004/jun/14/heritage.iraq (accessed 10 September 2024).
2 John O'Donohue, *Anam Cara* (Penguin, 2023).
3 Eugene Kennedy, *The Joy of Being Human: Reflections for Every Day of the Year* (Doubleday, 1976).
4 Thomas Merton, *No Man Is an Island* (Boston MA: Mariner Books, 2002).
5 Elie Wiesel, *A Passover Haggadah* (New York: Simon & Schuster, 1993).
6 C. S. Lewis, *The Lion, the Witch and the Wardrobe* (London: HarperCollins, 2009).

SESSION 5 SACRAMENTS AS A PLEDGE OF THE HOLY SPIRIT

1 Quotation attributed to John Stott.
2 Timothy Keller, *The Meaning of Marriage: Facing the Complexities of Commitment with the Wisdom of God* (London: Hodder & Stoughton, 2013).
3 See https://www.redletterchristians.org/what-if-jesus-meant-all-that-stuff/ (accessed 10 September 2024).
4 Quotation attributed to Billy Graham. See https://www.todayintheword.org/daily-devotional/pray-for-one-another (accessed 10 September 2024).
5 Dietrich Bonhoeffer, *The Cost of Discipleship* (London: SCM Press, 2015).
6 See https://www.puritanboard.com/threads/a-quote-from-augustine.2566/ (accessed 10 September 2024).
7 John L. Bell, *Orders for Personal Prayer*, Wild Goose Resource Group, www.wildgoose.scot.
8 A. W. Tozer, *How to be Filled with the Holy Spirit* (Eastford, CT: Martino Fine Books, 2010).

DR JANE WILLIAMS is the McDonald Professor in Christian Theology at St Mellitus College, London, and a visiting Lecturer at King's College London. Her recent books include *The Art of Christmas* (2021), *The Art of Advent* (2018), *Why Did Jesus Have to Die?* (2016, all SPCK), and *The Merciful Humility of God* (Bloomsbury, 2018).

PROFESSOR JAMES WALTERS is Director of the LSE Faith Centre.

DR SHARON PRENTIS is Deputy Director of the Racial Justice Unit.

This course can be downloaded digitally

OUR WARM THANKS to Monkeynut for recording and producing the course audio and video.

York Courses: https://spckpublishing.co.uk/bible-studies-and-group-resources/york-courses